Sports Illustrated KID$

ALL-STAR PICTURE PUZZLES

10

20

30

40

50

Sports Illustrated KIDS

ALL-STAR PICTURE PUZZLES

Featuring more than 70 action-packed photos from the world of sports!

PRODUCED BY

DOWNTOWN BOOKWORKS INC.

President Julie Merberg
Editor Sarah Parvis
Assistant Editor Kate Gibson

Special Thanks to: Sara Newberry, Patty Brown, Pam Abrams, Morris Katz, Nathanael Katz, Kal Katz, Janice Wilcoxson

Book Design and Puzzle Manipulation by
Brian Michael Thomas/**OUR HERO PRODUCTIONS**

SPORTS ILLUSTRATED KIDS

Managing Editor Bob Der
Creative Director Beth Power Bugler
Photo Editor Marguerite Schropp Lucarelli
Senior Editor Michael Northrop
Senior Art Director Edward Duarte
Assistant Photo Editor Gina Houseman

TIME INC. HOME ENTERTAINMENT

Publisher Richard Fraiman
General Manager Steven Sandonato
Executive Director, Marketing Services Carol Pittard
Director, Retail & Special Sales Tom Mifsud
Director, New Product Development Peter Harper
Assistant Director, Brand Marketing Laura Adam
Associate Counsel Helen Wan
Book Production Manager Jonathan Polsky
Design & Prepress Manager Anne-Michelle Gallero
Marketing Manager Alexandra Bliss

Special Thanks to: Bozena Bannett, Glenn Buonocore, Robert Marasco, Suzanne Janso, Brooke Reger, Mary Sarro-Waite, Ilene Schreider, Adriana Tierno, Alex Voznesenskiy

Answers to the cover puzzles:

JOHN BIEVER/SPORTS ILLUSTRATED

ROBERT BECK/SPORTS ILLUSTRATED

TABLE OF CONTENTS

HOW DO YOU SOLVE
A PICTURE PUZZLE? 6

ROOKIE
Warm-up Puzzles 8

ALL-STAR
The Ultimate Puzzle Workout 62

MVP
Championship Brainteasers  114

ANSWER KEY 156

HOW DO YOU SOLVE A PICTURE PUZZLE?

There are more than 70 picture puzzles in Sports Illustrated Kids *All-Star Picture Puzzles*. So grab a pencil or pen and get ready to tackle the ultimate collection of sports picture puzzles!

Every puzzle features two versions of an awesome sports photo. The pictures may look alike, but they are not the same. The second photo has been changed in at least six ways. One photo has twenty changes!

What sort of differences should you be on the lookout for? Uniforms might change color or shape. Team logos may grow, shrink, move, or rotate. Athletes may swap hats or trade equipment. Items on the field, the court, or in the stands might change size, shape, or color. Details might disappear. Keep your eye on the ball and watch out for animals or objects that might sneak into play.

The book is divided into three sections: Rookie, All-Star, and MVP. Each section is more difficult than the one before. The Rookie puzzles will get you warmed up. The All-Star level will get you in game shape, and the MVP puzzles will push you to top of your game.

Check out the example of a picture puzzle on the next page. It is from the All-Star chapter. You will find all kinds of changes in this puzzle.

FOR THE GLOVE OF THE GAME

Philadelphia Phillies second baseman Chase Utley takes the field.

ALL-STAR

The number of stars shows how tough a puzzle is. This one comes from the All-Star section, which is the medium level of difficulty.

AL TIELEMANS/SPORTS ILLUSTRATED

Some changes will be easy to spot, like this one. A baseball has been added to the player's glove.

SCORE

out of 8

Each time you spot a difference, circle it and put a check mark in one of the boxes. When all the boxes are filled, you've solved the puzzle!

Time Yourself!

This is the number of differences that can be found in the puzzle.

Keep an eye out for changing colors or things that have grown or shrunk. Here, the sign in the background has turned from blue to red and a section of the railing at the top of the stadium has been extended.

Some changes might be tough to see at first—like the decoration added to this player's uniform. Now he's a star!

To challenge yourself even more, grab a watch and time yourself. How fast can you find the changes?

The answers to each puzzle can be found in the Answer Key starting on page 156. Every change is circled in yellow.

WARMING UP

**We'll throw you some softballs to get you going. Be sure to keep your
eye on the ball, though. As you move further into the chapter, the puzzles
get more challenging!**

ROOKIE >>

CATCH ME IF YOU CAN

Kansas City shortstop Tony Pena royally tags Chone Figgins of the Los Angeles Angels.

Time Yourself!

ROOKIE

MEN IN BLACK

These refs had a ball during an NCAA basketball game.

ROOKIE

SMASH HIT

Maria Sharapova raises a racket at the 2007 French Open.

SCORE ☐☐☐☐☐☐☐ out of 7

Time Yourself!

ROOKIE ⭐

BOB MARTIN/SPORTS ILLUSTRATED

15

Wisconsin Badgers forward Brian Butch rises to the occasion against the Ohio State Buckeyes.

SCORE

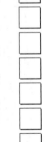

out of 7

Time Yourself!

Cincinnati Bengals quarterback Carson Palmer thinks over the game plan.

Sasha Cohen prepares for liftoff at the 2006 U.S. Figure Skating Championships.

ROOKIE

DAVID E. KLUTHO/SPORTS ILLUSTRATED

SCORE

☐
☐
☐
☐
☐
☐

out of 6

Time Yourself!

CROUCHING TIGER

Detroit Tigers catcher Ivan Rodriguez is poised behind the plate.

SCORE

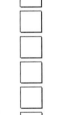

out of 7

Time Yourself!

OH, BROTHER!

Scott Niedermayer (27), then with the New Jersey Devils, battles his brother Rob (44), a center for the Anaheim Mighty Ducks, in the 2003 Stanley Cup Finals.

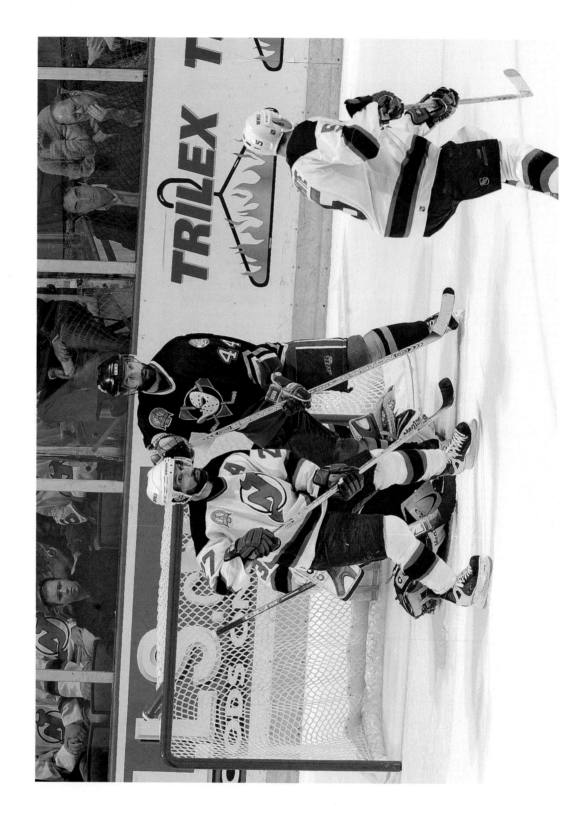

ROOKIE

An unflagging effort helps Nastia Liukin defend her All-Around title at the 2006 U.S. Gymnastics Championships.

ROOKIE

SCORE

out of 6

Time Yourself!

STICK IT TO 'EM

The University of Massachusetts upends Maryland in the semifinals of the 2006 NCAA lacrosse tournament.

SCORE

out of 8

Time Yourself!

AL TIELEMANS/SPORTS ILLUSTRATED

CAVALIER ATTITUDE

LeBron James of the Cleveland Cavaliers takes it to the hoop against the New Jersey Nets.

ROOKIE

SAUSAGES TO GO!

Though the pace isn't exactly sizzling, the "Sausage Race" is a popular tradition at Milwaukee Brewers games.

ROOKIE

JOHN BIEVER/SPORTS ILLUSTRATED

DOWNHILL DYNAMO

U.S. skier Bode Miller speeds down the mountain during a World Cup event.

JOLLY ROGER

Swiss superstar Roger Federer cruises to his fourth straight U.S. Open title in 2007.

ROOKIE

HEAVENLY VIEW

Los Angeles Angels outfielder Vladimir Guerrero comes out swinging against the Cleveland Indians.

Time Yourself!

ROOKIE

PUZZLING PILEUP

The Ohio State Buckeyes get tough against the Washington Huskies.

Time Yourself!

ROOKIE ⭐

The runners are right on track in the women's 100-meter hurdles
at the 2007 World Championships in Osaka, Japan.

 ROOKIE

SCORE

out of 6

Time Yourself!

40

BMX BANDIT

A biker takes to the air during a BMX vert event on the 2007 AST Dew Tour.

SCORE

out of 6

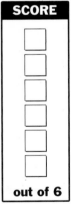

Time Yourself!

HATS OFF

The Japanese team shows some class at the 2007 Little League World Series in Williamsport, Pennsylvania.

Time Yourself!

ROOKIE

RUN FOR THE ROSES

The pack thunders down the track at the 2007 Kentucky Derby.

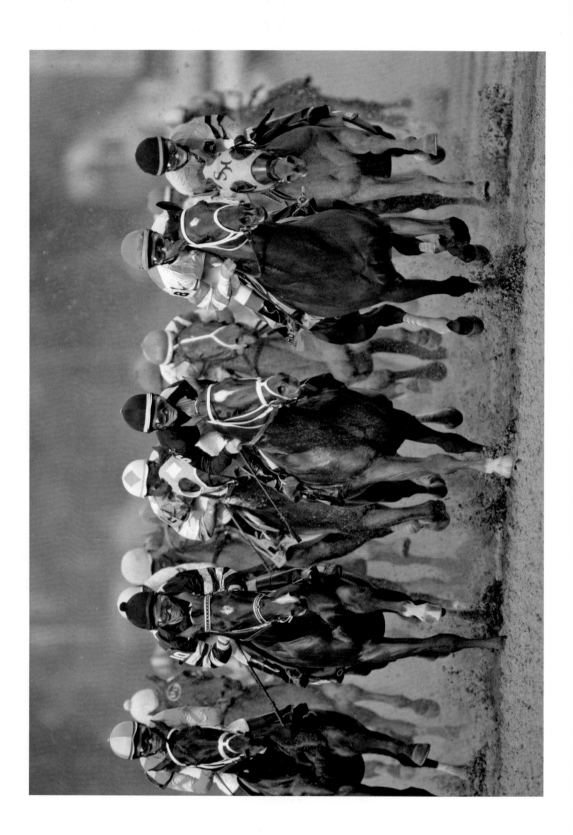

DIRT DEVILS

Motocross riders kick up some dust at Summer X Games 12 in Los Angeles.

ROOKIE

CAPTURE THE FLAG

At the University of Maryland, flag football is a full-contact sport.

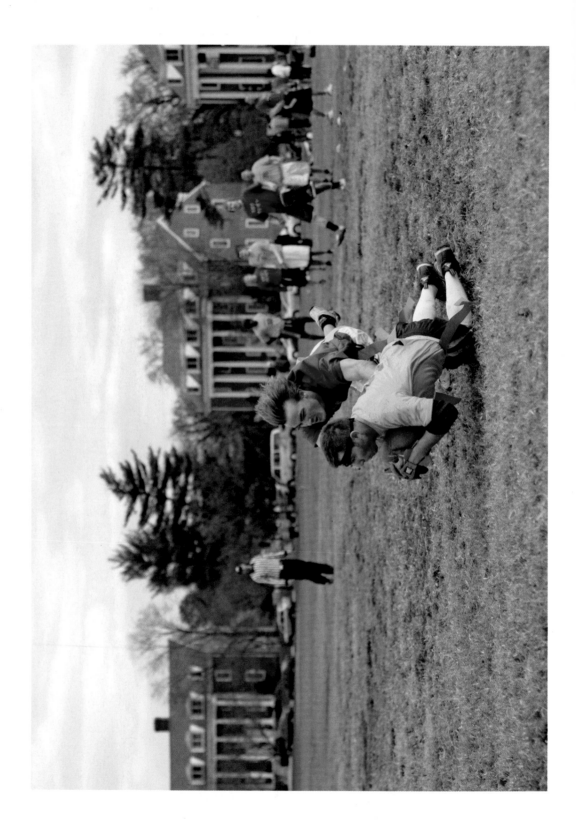

ROOKIE ★

VROOM WITH A VIEW

Jeff Gordon puts the pedal to the metal at California Speedway.

ROOKIE ★

SLIPPING THROUGH THE D

Minnesota Lynx guard Seimone Augustus gives it her best shot against the Detroit Shock's tight defense.

ROOKIE

DON'T GO BATTY

The Philadelphia Phillies and Cincinnati Reds swung special pink bats during a Mother's Day showdown.

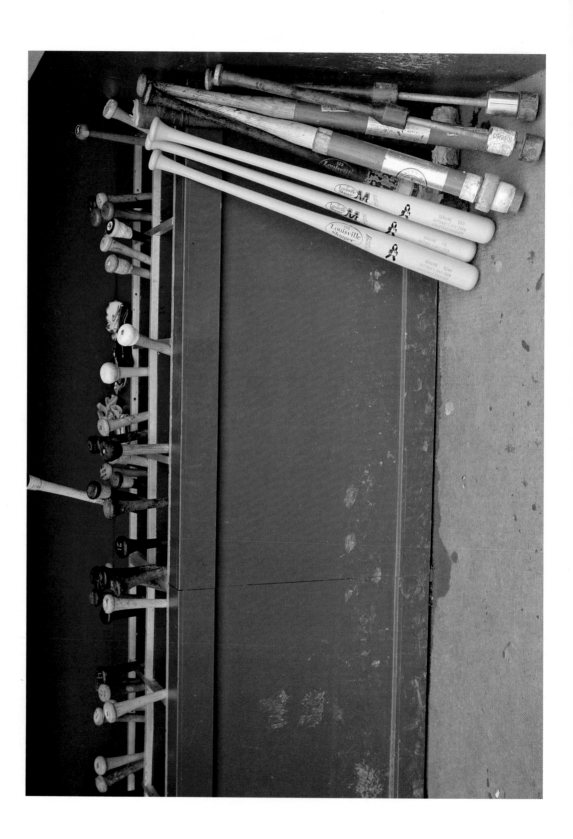

Time Yourself!

ROOKIE

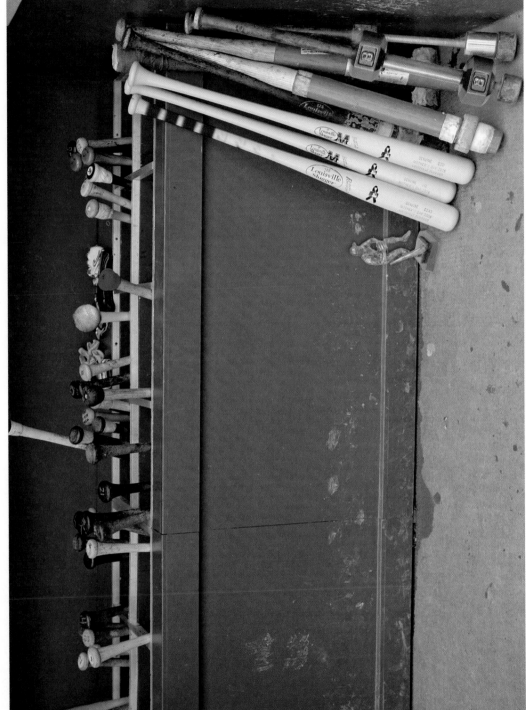

TOO CLOSE FOR COMFORT

Maureen Mmadu of Nigeria almost got a kick out of this play by Sweden's Victoria Svensson during the 2007 Women's World Cup.

Time Yourself!

ROOKIE

SCORE out of 6

SIMON BRUTY/SPORTS ILLUSTRATED

57

RUSH HOUR

Running back Shaun Alexander of the Seattle Seahawks makes a break for it against the Chicago Bears.

ROOKIE

THE U.S. A-TEAM

Superstar "benchwarmers" LeBron James, Carmelo Anthony, and Kobe Bryant take a break during a U.S. national team game.

ROOKIE

READY FOR THE BIG LEAGUES?
Think you've got the hang of it? The tricky puzzles in this chapter will really put your skills to the test.

ALL-STAR>>

BELLY FLOP

Goalie Ray Emery of the Ottawa Senators goes all out during the 2007 Stanley Cup Finals.

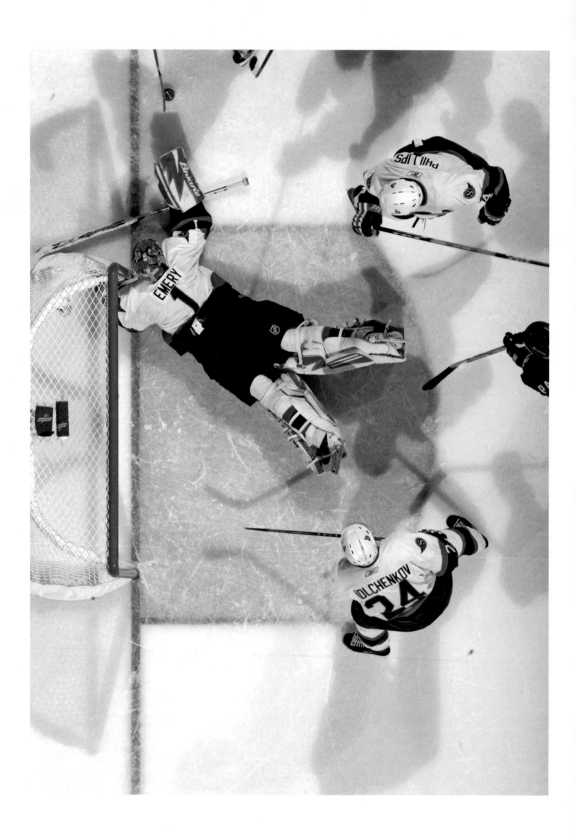

Time Yourself!

ALL-STAR

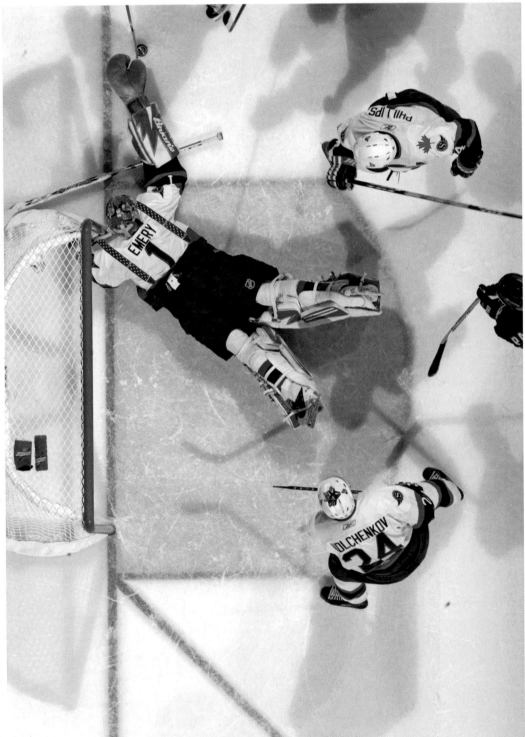

FUMBLE!

The Cleveland Browns and Pittsburgh Steelers scramble for a loose ball.

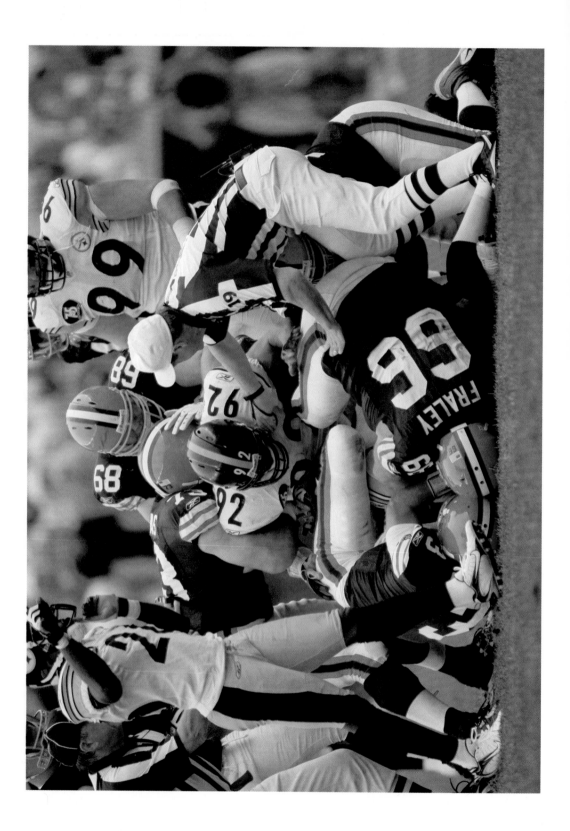

ALL-
STAR

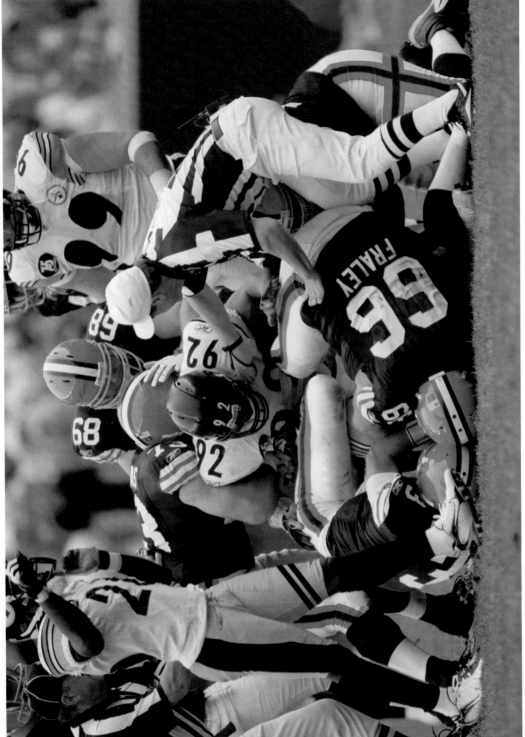

AL TIELEMANS/SPORTS ILLUSTRATED

OOF!

Swin Cash of the Detroit Shock fights through—or, well, into—a screen by Rebekkah Brunson of the Sacramento Monarchs.

ALL-
STAR

ON A ROLL

Three racers take it right down to the wire during the All-American Soap Box Derby.

ALL-STAR

PUT ON ICE

Center Robert Lang of the Detroit Red Wings gets tripped up by defenseman Brad Stuart of the Calgary Flames.

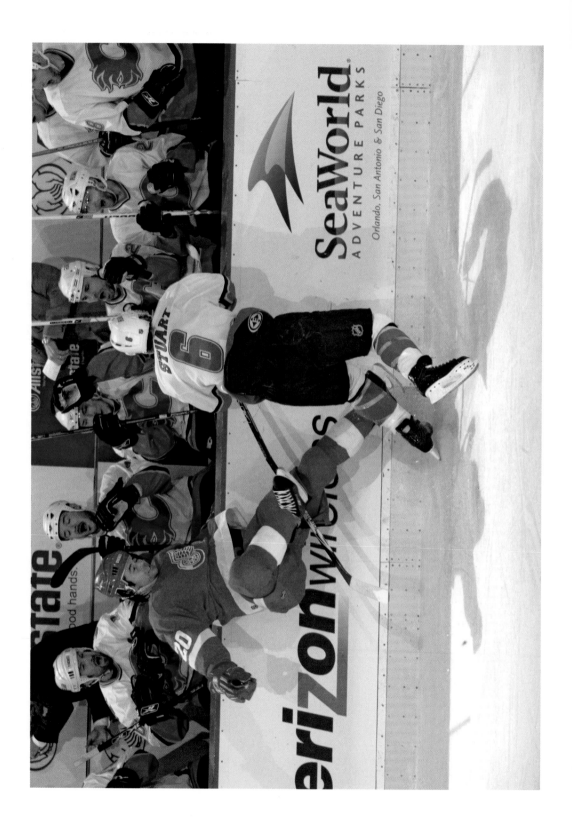

Time Yourself!

ALL-
STAR

Horses and their riders take the leap during a steeplechase event in England.

ALL-
STAR

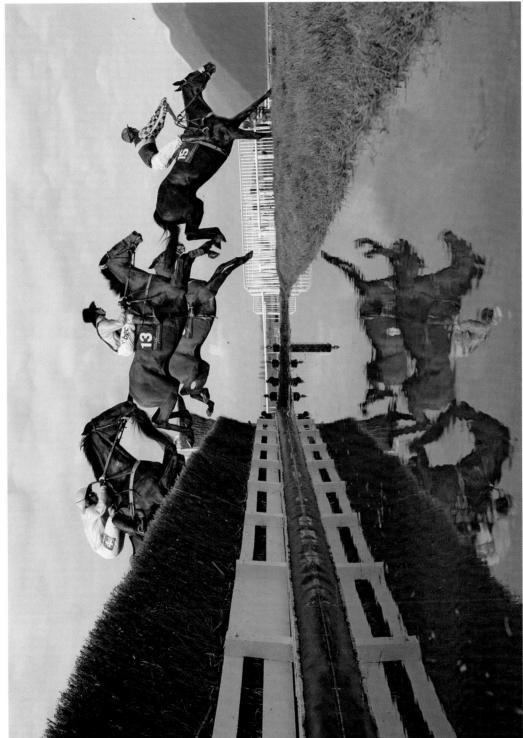

BATTER UP!

Mets third baseman David Wright gets in the swing of things against the Florida Marlins.

Time Yourself!

ALL-STAR

MONSTER MASH

A metallic beast roars into action at a monster truck show.

SCORE

out of 8

ALL-STAR

I'LL PASS

Arizona Cardinals quarterback Kurt Warner attempts to air it out against the San Diego Chargers.

Time Yourself!

ALL-
STAR

These runners go the distance at the 2007 IAAF Athletics World Championships.

ALL-STAR

SCORE

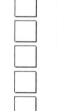

out of 8

Time Yourself!

Michael Phelps and the rest of the field dive right in during the men's 200-meter individual medley at the 2007 World Championships.

ALL-STAR

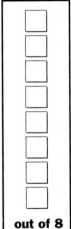

SCORE

out of 8

Time Yourself!

HEINZ KLUETMEIER/SPORTS ILLUSTRATED

SWING TIME

Pro golfer Sean O'Hair shows some drive at The Players Championship in 2007.

Time Yourself!

ALL-STAR

ROBERT BECK/SPORTS ILLUSTRATED

FOR THE GLOVE OF THE GA

Philadelphia Phillies second baseman Chase Utley takes the field.

Time Yourself!

ALL-
STAR

PRESTO CHANGE-O

The 48 team springs into action as NASCAR star Jimmie Johnson pulls in for a pit stop.

ALL-
STAR

Wisconsin cheerleaders and fans show their support for the Badgers during a men's basketball game.

Time Yourself!

ALL-
STAR

BM-EXCELLENT

A rider flips out during a BMX dirt event on the 2007 AST Dew Tour.

ALL-
STAR

THROUGH THE ROOF

The U.S. men's basketball team talks it over during an Olympic qualifying game against Canada.

ALL-
STAR

The Philadelphia Phillies make themselves at home in the visitors' dugout at Busch Stadium in St. Louis.

DAVID E. KLUTHO/SPORTS ILLUSTRATED

ALL-
STAR

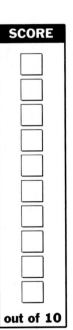

SCORE

out of 10

Time Yourself!

STICK 'EM UP

Friends Academy gets it together during a high school lacrosse game in Manhasset, New York.

Time Yourself!

ALL-
STAR

Players from Georgia (U.S.) and Japan have a ball at the 2007 Little League World Series championship game.

ALL-
STAR

**USC isn't horsing around when it comes to its mascot:
Here's Traveler and his trusty rider Tommy Trojan.**

**ALL-
STAR**

SCORE

out of 9

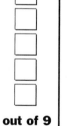

Time Yourself!

Memphis mascot Pouncer gets the team psyched before tip-off.

ALL-STAR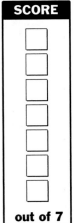

SCORE

out of 7

Time Yourself!

WE HAVE LIFTOFF

Fans take in some high-flying action at a monster truck show.

HOME PLATE DUSTUP

Toronto Blue Jays catcher Jason Phillips tags out Boston Red Sox slugger David Ortiz at Fenway Park.

SCORE

out of 8

ALL-
STAR

HAWKISH DEFENSE

Charlotte Bobcats forward Adam Morrison encounters some stiff resistance on his way to the hoop against the Atlanta Hawks.

Time Yourself!

ALL-STAR

SUNSET STRATEGY

Atlanta Falcons linemen get their marching orders before a game.

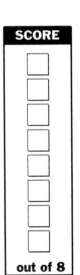

SCORE

out of 8

Time Yourself!

PUMP UP THE VOL-UME

Tennessee Vols fans show some school spirit during a football game.

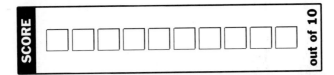

Time Yourself!

ALL-STAR

ROBERT BECK/SPORTS ILLUSTRATED

CHAMPIONSHIP TIME!
You've made it to the picture puzzle playoffs. The puzzles in this chapter are the most challenging yet—the last one has 20 changes!

HOT WHEELS

Marcel Hug of Switzerland leads the pack in the men's 1500-meter wheelchair event at the 2007 IAAF Athletics World Championships.

MVP

GOOOOOOAL!

Detroit Red Wings winger Tomas Holmstrom celebrates after scoring a goal against the San Jose Sharks.

Time Yourself!

MVP

OPENING DAY

The stars (and stripes) are out for the Washington Nationals' Opening Day at RFK Stadium.

SCORE

out of 10

MVP

121

NO KIDDING:

Guard Jason Kidd dishes the ball as the U.S. national team takes on Canada.

MVP

POSITIVELY BEAMING

Chellsie Memmel soars above the balance beam during the 2006 U.S. Gymnastics Championships.

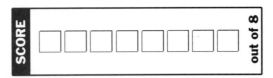

MVP

RIGHT OUT OF THE GATE

Some of the fastest horses in the world burst from the gate at the 2007 Preakness Stakes.

MVP

ALL STITCHED UP

A basket of baseballs await their fate at Yankee Stadium in the Bronx, New York.

MVP

GATOR-AID

These Florida football fans are blue even when the Gators win.

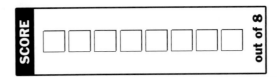

MVP

JAZZ HANDS

The Utah Jazz get defensive against the Los Angeles Clippers.

Time Yourself!

MVP

TIGER SIGHTING

Fans clamor for a glimpse of Tiger Woods as he putts during the 2006 British Open.

Time Yourself!

MVP

THE SKY'S THE LIMIT

No one was bored during this skateboard vert event on the 2007 AST Dew Tour.

MVP

The field revs it up for a packed motocross event at Summer X Games 12 in Los Angeles.

MVP

SCORE

out of 8

Time Yourself!

FUZZY PHOTO

A menagerie of mascots turned the 2007 NHL All-Star Celebration into a real zoo.

SCORE

out of 10

MVP

BAND TOGETHER

The LSU band pumps up the volume at a Tigers football game.

MVP

SCORE

out of 9

Time Yourself!

MAKING AN ENTRANCE

Eagles mascot Swoop takes the field in Philly.

Time Yourself!

MVP

WATER YOU WAITING FOR?

Swimmer Kate Ziegler launches herself into the 400-meter freestyle event at the U.S. National Championships.

MVP

QUIET, PLEASE

The gallery gets a good look at the action at the The Players Championship in 2007.

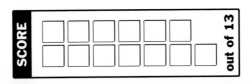

SCORE

out of 13

MVP

A GRAND ENTRANCE

The Florida Gators take the field.

Time Yourself!

MVP

HERE IT COMES!

Tennis star Serena Williams serves one up at the 2007 French Open.

Time Yourself!

MVP

The Red Sox celebrate after rocking the Colorado Rockies in the 2007 World Series.

Time Yourself!

MVP

ANSWER KEY
Ready to see how you did? The changes to each puzzle
are circled in yellow.

Page 10–11
Catch Me If You Can

Page 12–13
Men in Black

Page 14–15
Smash Hit

Page 16–17
Seeing Red

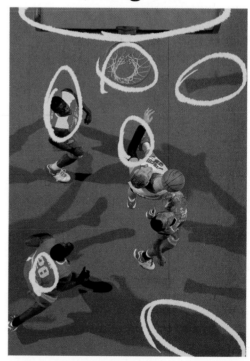

ANSWERS

Page 18—19
Carson Close-up

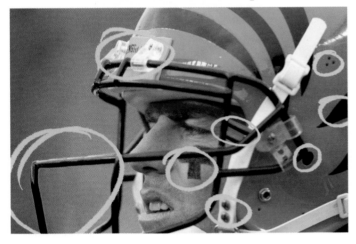

Page 20—21
Skate Expectations

Page 22—23
Crouching Tiger

Page 24—25
Oh, Brother!

Page 26
Leaping Liukin

Page 27
Stick It to 'Em

Page 28–29
Cavalier Attitude

Page 30–31
Sausages to Go!

Page 32–33
Downhill Dynamo

Page 34–35
Jolly Roger

Page 36–37
Heavenly View

Page 38–39
Puzzling Pileup

Page 40
And They're Off!

Page 41
BMX Bandit

Page 42–43
Hats Off

Page 44–45
Run for the Roses

Page 46–47
Dirt Devils

Page 48–49
Capture the Flag

Page 50–51
Vroom with a View

Page 52–53
Slipping through the D

Page 54–55
Don't Go Batty

Page 56–57
Too Close for Comfort

Page 58–59
Rush Hour

Page 60–61
The U.S. A-Team

Page 64—65
Belly Flop

Page 66—67
Fumble!

Page 68—69
Oof!

Page 70—71
On a Roll

ANSWERS

Page 72–73
Put on Ice

Page 74–75
Hold Your Horses

Page 76–77
Batter Up!

Page 78–79
Monster Mash

Page 80–81
I'll Pass

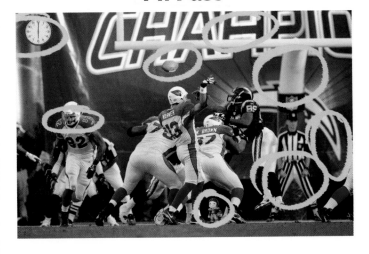

Page 82
Leaders of the Pack

Page 83
Pooling Their Talent

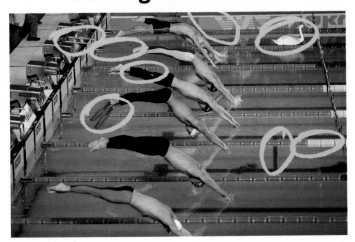

Page 84–85
Swing Time

Page 86–87
For the Glove of the Game

Page 88–89
Presto Change-O

Page 90–91
Well Red

Page 92–93
BM-Excellent

Page 142–143
Band Together

Page 144–145
Making an Entrance

Page 146–147
Water You Waiting for?

Page 148–149
Quiet, Please

ANSWERS

Page 150–151
A Grand Entrance

Page 152–153
Here It Comes!

Page 154–155
Boston Sweep Party

176